FOLLOW
THE TRAIL

A young person's guide to the great outdoors

Jessica Loy

Henry Holt and Company
New York

Dedicated to
Emma and Lydia
for all their great contributions

Thanks to Europa Baker, Zachary Herman,
Bobby O'Connor, Jennifer Rosenbaum, and especially Tom Santelli
for their patience; Nick Lyons for his wisdom;
Christy Ottaviano and Martha Rago for all their hard work;
and my family for their lifelong support.

Henry Holt and Company, LLC
Publishers since 1866
115 West 18th Street
New York, New York 10011
www.henryholt.com

Henry Holt is a registered trademark of Henry Holt and Company, LLC
Copyright © 2003 by Jessica Loy. All rights reserved.
Distributed in Canada by H. B. Fenn and Company Ltd.

Library of Congress Cataloging-in-Publication Data
Loy, Jessica.
Follow the trail: a young person's guide to the great outdoors / Jessica Loy.
p. cm.
Summary: A beginner's guide to camping and hiking, including what gear to bring,
how to keep safe, and how to have fun.
Contents: Camping—Planning—Packing—Setting up camp—Camp chores—Safety—
Hiking—Animal tracks—Tracking—Leaves and trees—Flowers—Animals—Birds—
Clouds—Rainy days—Campfires—Time to eat—Games—Constellations—
Night sounds—Time to go.
1. Outdoor recreation for children—Juvenile literature.
[1. Outdoor recreation. 2. Camping. 3. Hiking. 4. Nature study.] I. Title.
GV191.63.L69 2003 796.54—dc21 2002068911

ISBN 0-8050-6195-9 / First Edition—2003
Printed in the United States of America on acid-free paper. ∞
1   3   5   7   9   10   8   6   4   2

The artist used a combination of computer-generated illustrations,
photography, and acrylic paint. The children's drawings were created by
Emma and Lydia Loy-Santelli, using crayons and markers.

Contents

Camping

Camping is an exciting adventure because you never know what will happen or whom you may see. That's what makes living outdoors so much fun.

Meet **Emma** and her little sister, **Lydia.**

They're taking three good friends—

Bobby,

Europa,

and Zachary—

on a camping trip to one of their favorite sites. Emma and Lydia love to camp and hope their friends will like it, too. This book is full of tips to help you get started on your own camping trip.

So let's go!

Planning

Planning your trip comes first. There are several important decisions you and your group will need to make:

1. Where should we go?
- Private Campground
- State Park
- Wilderness Site

2. When do we go?
- Spring
- Summer
- Fall

3. How will we get there?
- Car
- Canoe
- Hike

4. Where do we sleep?
- Tent
- Lean-to
- Camper

If you've never camped before, try something simple, like car camping in a private campground with bathroom and shower facilities. There are many environmental groups that offer camping trips for families. State parks provide campgrounds close to home. And don't forget—there is always your own backyard!

Consider all the variables. For instance, backpacking to a site will limit how much you are able to carry, while a canoe trip requires experienced canoeing and good water safety skills. Different seasons mean different challenges, such as biting insects, abundant rain, cold, or drought. Check out your destination before scheduling a trip.

Wherever you go and however you get there, try to live as close to nature as possible. Sleep in a tent, a lean-to, or better yet sleep out under the stars and feel the dew tickle your nose when you wake up in the morning. It's a wonderful experience!

Packing

Packing depends a lot on how and where you travel. Remember, you can carry more in a car than in a backpack, and a canoe trip will require different things altogether. Here is a list of items just about every camper needs. Feel free to add your own extras, but don't overpack!

General List

- cooking items
- picnic tarp
- stove and fuel
- matches
- water jugs
- purifying tablets
- shovel
- lantern / flashlight
- first-aid kit
- insect repellent
- sunblock
- nylon cord
- trash bags
- toilet paper
- biodegradable soap
- biodegradable dish detergent
- space blanket
- fresh batteries
- maps and guidebooks
- compass

General Equipment

You may or may not require a tent, but you will always want to eat. Your menu and the number of people in your group will determine your needs. A smart packing list usually includes a frying pan, large pot, spatula, and a mess kit for each person (utensils, plate, bowl, and small cup). Your food choices should be nutritious, energizing, and lightweight (see page 36). You may want to bring a picnic tarp to eat under in the rain. If campfires are not permitted, you will need a camp stove and fuel. Stoves save the environment and cook faster. A good supply of matches is important. Water is essential—individual water bottles as well as larger storage containers. Collapsible water jugs are very portable. If the water supply is questionable, it's wise to use purifying tablets or a filtration system. Tablets can often make the water taste funny, so Emma and Lydia like to add a powdered drink mix to it. A shovel is handy for digging latrines. Flashlights are always convenient, but lanterns illuminate a larger area without needing to be held. A first-aid kit should be well stocked and include a polyethylene space blanket for emergency warmth. Insect repellent and sunblock go without saying! Nylon cord is great for clotheslines and bear bags, and don't forget a few trash bags to carry out your garbage.

Personal Equipment

Personal items can also vary depending on your specific needs and the type of trip you are taking. Eliminate extras that add weight and are not necessary for your safety and comfort, but remember to bring a toothbrush and maybe your favorite stuffed animal. Good hiking boots are always a must, even if you don't do a lot of walking; wilderness areas are full of uneven surfaces and your ankles can use the support. Wool or thermal socks and liners keep blisters away and feet comfortable. Bring along sneakers or moccasins for in-camp relaxing and water shoes if you want to swim or wade. Bandannas can wipe a sweaty brow and keep mosquitoes away; a hat will block out the sun. If you are in high altitude or camping off-season, bring along mittens and a wool hat; this may seem unnecessary, but wilderness areas can be much colder than your backyard. A wool or fleece sweater is important, and don't forget good rainwear—preferably a rain jacket and rain pants. You want to be as comfortable as you can at all times so the trip stays fun. A whistle is an essential safety item for each person to carry; the sound will travel much farther than your voice. A pocketknife is often useful but can be dangerous; make sure you learn the right way to work with one. A windbreaker goes a long way when trying to stay warm, but if you run out of room, a rain jacket will do just fine. Lastly, carry a notebook or journal to keep notes on the trip.

Personal List

- toothbrush / toothpaste
- hiking boots
- socks and liners
- camp shoes
- bandannas
- sun hat

- mittens / wool hat
- wool / fleece sweater
- rain gear
- whistles
- pocketknife
- windbreaker
- journal
- sturdy shorts
- sturdy long pants
- short- / long-sleeve shirts
- bathing suit
- towel
- 1-liter water bottle
- sleeping bag / pad
- emergency candle
- games / stuffed toys
- camera and film
- sunglasses

P.S. Our list covers the basics, so if you are trying a new kind of camping adventure and are not sure what you will need, ask an experienced camper or find a guide with a detailed equipment list for your particular outing.

Set Up Camp

Set Up Camp as soon as you reach your campsite. A good camper never gets caught in the dark without a place to sleep.

Start by going over the campground rules concerning fires, garbage, bathroom facilities, and other important environmental matters. If you are in a wilderness area, you'll have to establish some of your own rules. The first rule that every camper should follow is leave-no-trace. There should be no evidence of your stay.

Ideally, choose a campsite near water, preferably in a clearing in the woods that's neither directly under trees nor on an open plain. Find a spot with adequate space for a tent, fire ring and camp stove, bear bag, and latrine, using the distance rules on this page.

Organize your cooking near the camp stove and use wood scraps to make a tabletop for preparing meals. Keep unused food in secured storage containers or hang a bear bag (see page 12). A stream makes a great cooler as long as your containers are well sealed and anchored. Also, set up a dishwashing area near a flat rock or tree stump where you can put things out to dry. When the campsite is well organized, the whole camping experience is more fun.

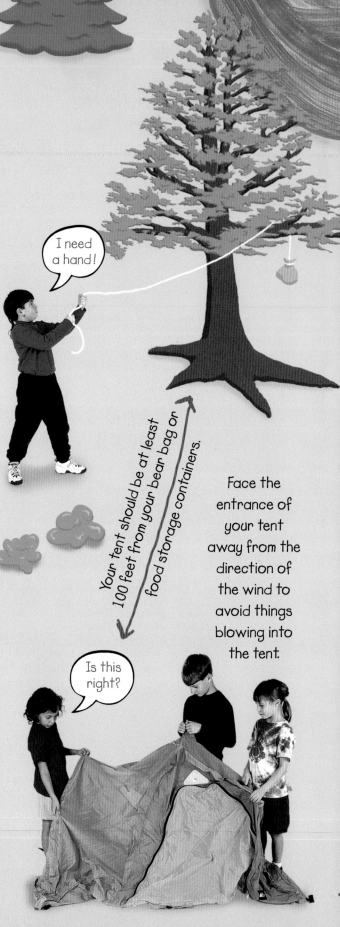

I need a hand!

Your tent should be at least 100 feet from your bear bag or food storage containers.

Face the entrance of your tent away from the direction of the wind to avoid things blowing into the tent.

Is this right?

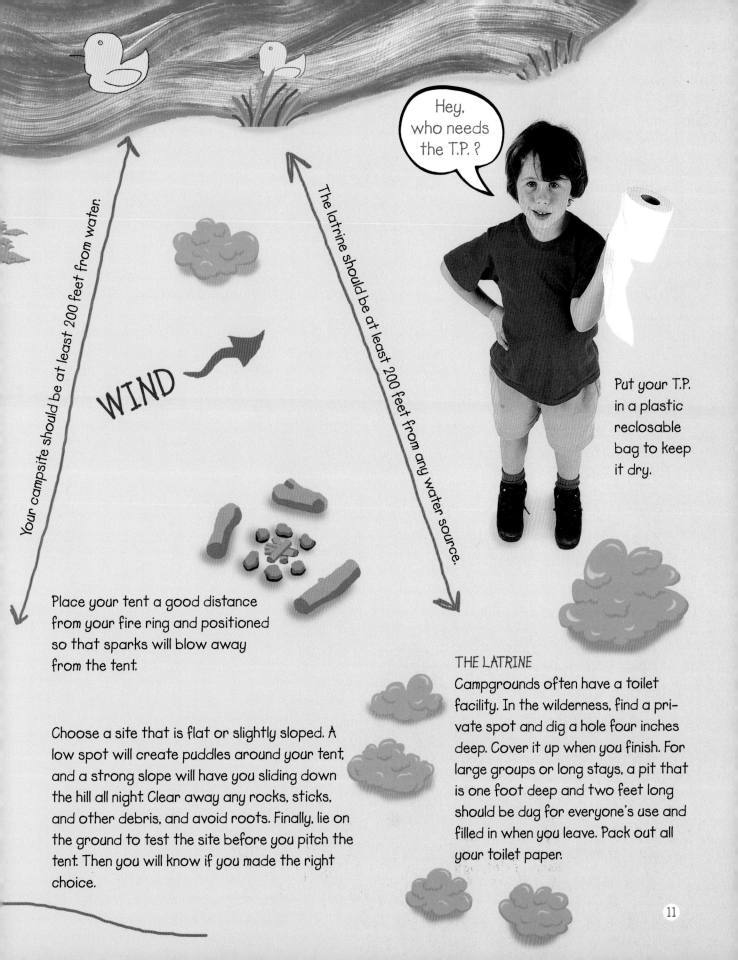

Your campsite should be at least 200 feet from water.

The latrine should be at least 200 feet from any water source.

WIND

Hey, who needs the T.P. ?

Put your T.P. in a plastic reclosable bag to keep it dry.

Place your tent a good distance from your fire ring and positioned so that sparks will blow away from the tent.

Choose a site that is flat or slightly sloped. A low spot will create puddles around your tent, and a strong slope will have you sliding down the hill all night. Clear away any rocks, sticks, and other debris, and avoid roots. Finally, lie on the ground to test the site before you pitch the tent. Then you will know if you made the right choice.

THE LATRINE
Campgrounds often have a toilet facility. In the wilderness, find a private spot and dig a hole four inches deep. Cover it up when you finish. For large groups or long stays, a pit that is one foot deep and two feet long should be dug for everyone's use and filled in when you leave. Pack out all your toilet paper.

Camp Chores

are important for a healthy, comfortable trip, and if everyone works together the tasks can be both fun and fast.

String a hanging line between two trees for your wet towels and clothes. Sweep your tent each morning, and air out your sleeping bags on the line.

Washing dishes is a great time to tell stories when two people share the work. During dinner, heat a pot of water over the fire or on the stove. Later, use the heated water for washing and a second pot of cold water to rinse. A dish towel is useful for quick drying.

Put away all food when there are scavengers, such as bears or raccoons, in the area. Campgrounds sometimes provide storage boxes. Otherwise hang a bear bag, with a sturdy rope.

The bear bag should be at least 10 feet off the ground and well away from the tree trunk. Use a miller's knot (page 33) to secure the bag.

Collect water away from the edge of a stream or lake and avoid stagnant water. Always get water with a buddy watching and be careful; stream bottoms and rocks can be slippery.

Emma's Notes

I'm in charge of making the chore chart. It's easy!
Take a piece of notebook paper and list all the chores along
the top and the days you will be camping along the side. Give
each person a different chore for each day. Don't forget
that some chores, like cooking and dishwashing, are better
for two people to do together. I like to decorate our chart
with a colorful border.

Emma, did you hear that chipmunk this morning?

Set up and dispose of dishwashing water
away from any natural water source and
always use biodegradable soaps. Also, try
not to disturb fragile plants and mosses.

Safety First—always.

There are many potential dangers when camping, but if you know what those dangers are and follow sensible rules, everyone will be at ease.

1. Snakes. Research what kinds of snakes live in your camping area and what they look like. Snakes are very shy and would rather avoid you. And you should avoid them, too, because a few are poisonous.

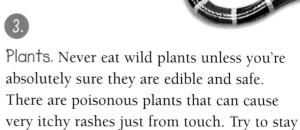

2. Hiking. Never take even a short hike without proper supplies. Know what is needed in an emergency and plan for bad weather and difficult terrain. Respect the wilderness; be prepared for the worst and you will always be ready.

3.

Plants. Never eat wild plants unless you're absolutely sure they are edible and safe. There are poisonous plants that can cause very itchy rashes just from touch. Try to stay on established paths and trails to avoid these unfriendly plants, but also be sure you know what they look like.

FIRST-AID KIT:

You can buy a prepared first-aid kit or make your own using the list below. Be sure to put everything in a plastic bag so the contents stay dry.

- Band-Aids
- Sterile gauze pads and athletic tape
- Moleskin for blisters
- Small scissors
- Tweezers for splinters
- Aspirin for aches and pains
- Antihistamine tablets for insect bites or other allergic reactions
- Antibiotic cream to disinfect wounds
- Safety pins to hold together bandages or torn clothes
- Wide elastic wrap for sprained ankles
- Snake-bite kit
- Space blanket

Poison Oak has three green shiny leaflets that are hairy underneath. Berries are cream colored.

Poison Ivy has three shiny green leaflets with smooth or teethlike edges. Berries are cream colored.

Poison Sumac has smooth compound leaflets that grow in a V shape from the stem. It also has drooping white berries.

4.

Sun. If you are hiking long distances under a hot sun, have plenty of liquids to replenish the water that is leaving your body through perspiration. Put on a hat, seek shade in the middle of the day, and always wear sunscreen. Remember, with every 1,000 feet of elevation gain, the sun becomes 4 percent more intense.

Whew, that sun is hot!

Deer Tick

actual size

Brown Dog Tick

actual size

5. Water. It is safest to bring your own water. If you need to drink water from a stream, carry either bacteria-killing water tablets or a water filter, or be prepared to boil all drinking water. Camping stores sell a variety of options for keeping your water safe.

6. Ticks. Get into the habit of regularly checking yourself for ticks. These insects are usually picked up in tall grass or brush. Some ticks carry Lyme disease, which makes it important to know what they look like and how to properly remove them from your skin.

7. Lost. Stay where you are and call for help. Blowing a whistle is an even better way of getting attention, so tie one to your backpack.

8.

Fire. Almost all camping trips involve some element of fire, and both your belongings and the environment around you are very flammable: BE CARE-FUL, PLEASE! Fire should be handled only under adult supervision and should be kept away from tents and other flammable materials. Use flashlights and battery-powered lights as often as possible to avoid accidents. (See page 35 for more campfire safety tips.)

9. Bears. Like snakes, bears are shy and would prefer not to be seen. However, they are likely to forget their shyness when they smell food. You should never have food in your tent (including toothpaste), and if bears are about, use a hanging bear bag (see page 12) to store your supplies. Observe bears from a distance, avoid a mother bear with cubs, and always back away slowly while facing the bear, if you do encounter one.

Hiking offers you a chance to explore. Before you start, prepare a daypack, proper footgear, food, and safety supplies. Everyone can take turns leading, reading the map, and using a compass. Your map should clearly show the area you will be hiking. Topographic wilderness maps define terrain, outstanding landmarks (such as lakes, trails, and roads), and directional points. By locating north, you can coordinate a map with your compass and find where you are on the map. For example, if you climb a mountain, a map and compass can help identify distant points of interest.

Hey, we found the trail, Emma!

Emma's Notes

Get out your notebook and try making a map of your campsite. Indicate the location of trails, streams, roads, your tent, the best climbing tree, and other important places. Then see if everyone else can follow it. Draw a compass rose and indicate north.

A mileage line is used to determine distance on a map. Copy the line length onto a piece of paper and move it along end-to-end between points of interest to find out how many miles apart they are.

A compass is useful for identifying your location and nearby landmarks on a map, but first you need to know which direction is north. A map always indicates north.

Topographic lines or rings indicate elevation. The closer together the lines are, the steeper the grade.

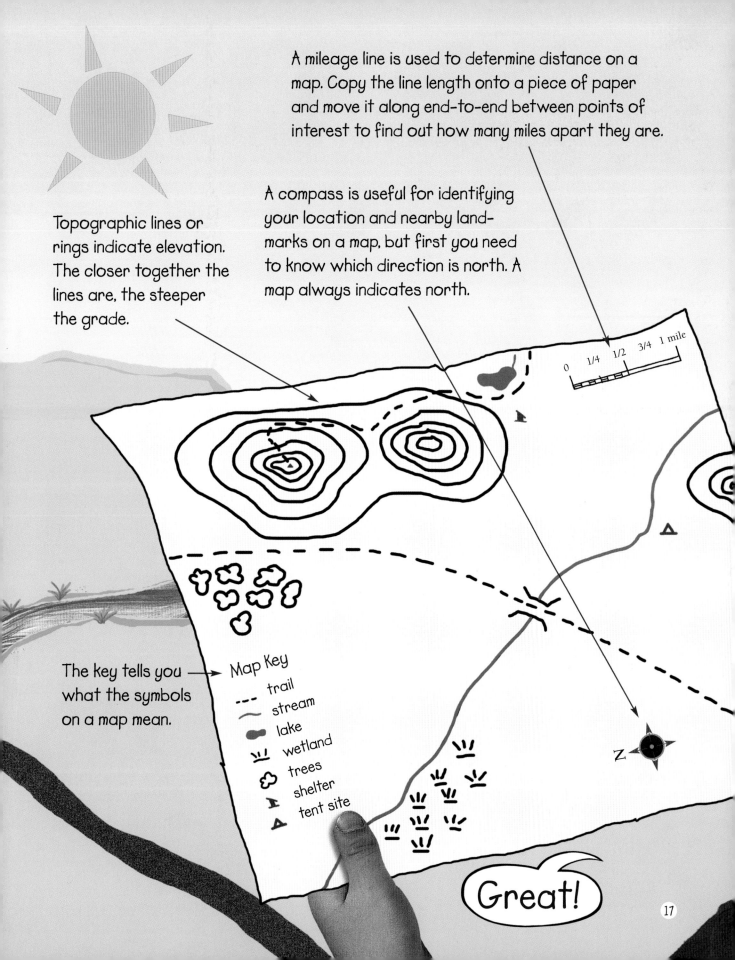

0   1/4   1/2   3/4   1 mile

The key tells you what the symbols on a map mean.

Map Key

- - - trail
~ stream
lake
wetland
trees
shelter
tent site

Z

Great!

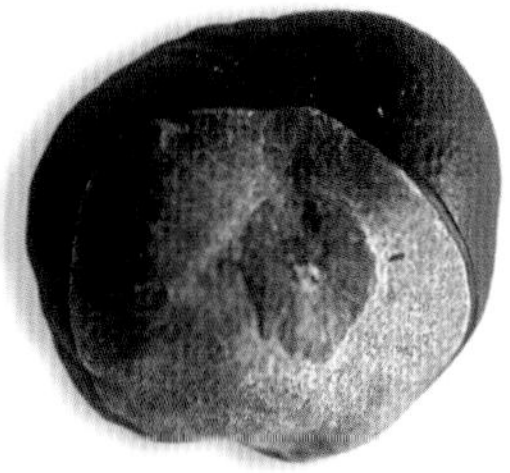

Chestnut

Beechnut Pod

Red Oak Acorn

Elm leaves are double-toothed and uneven. The tree's inner bark is tough enough to use for fishing line.

Black Oak leaves look like Red Oak, but are shinier.

Silver Maple leaves are silver underneath.

Trees are all around us, so it's interesting to learn the names of some familiar trees that can be seen both in your neighborhood and in the woods. Most trees are easily identifiable by their leaves, but others also have very distinctive bark, cones, flowers, and seeds. Here are some of our easy-to-find favorites.

Here's a great leaf for the notebook.

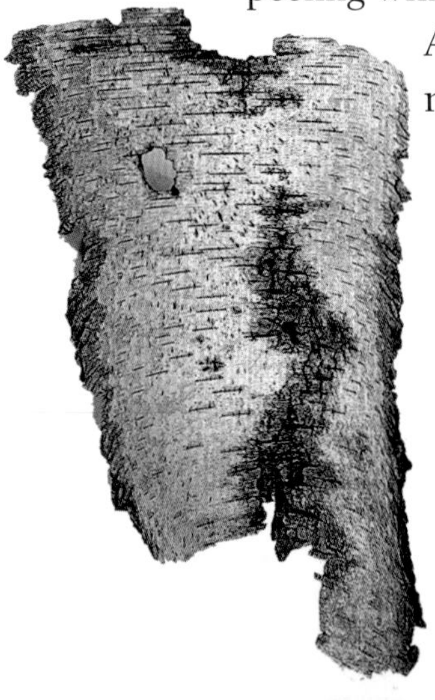

Paper Birch Bark is distinctive because of its peeling white bark, which Native Americans used to make canoes and wigwams.

Paper Birch has double-toothed leaves that are dark green on top.

Spruce trees have short, stiff, sharp four-sided needles.

Spruce Cone

Hemlock trees have flat, soft, round-tipped needles.

White Pine needles are two to four inches long, bunched in groups of five. All pine needles grow in clusters.

White Pine Cone

Cedar trees have tiny leaf scales arranged in flat fan shapes.

Sugar Maple trees produce sap that is used to make maple syrup.

Red Maple trees have bright red flowers, twigs, and buds.

Beech trees have distinctive smooth gray bark and leaves that are hairless and have small teeth.

Maple Rubbing by Lydia!

An idea from Lydia!

I like to pick up leaves when I'm hiking or sitting at our campsite. It's fun to trace the leaf shapes in my notebook and identify them with a tree guide. I also make rubbings of leaves with a crayon or pencil. You can really see the veins and textures of a leaf by doing a rubbing.

Wildflowers

add a splash of color to the natural world. Some plants are native to an area, while others travel as seeds on the wind, or on animals, birds, and even people from faraway places. A wildflower guide will help you identify the many pretty faces you come across on the trail.

Black-eyed Susan grows in fields and open woods. Its origins are in the Midwest.

Chicory flower closes by midday, and its roots are sometimes used in coffee or as a coffee substitute.

Red Clover originally came from Europe and is sometimes used as a medicinal tea.

Bird's-foot Trefoil is named for the bird-foot appearance of the flowers after they go to seed.

Milkweed attracts monarch butterfly larvae who eat the plant's poisonous leaves, which prevents birds from eating them.

Purple Loosestrife is a beautiful flower that is found in many wetlands. Many environmental groups in America are trying to remove this invasive foreigner because it's choking out native plants.

Bull Thistle is very pretty, but like all thistles it has very sharp spikes, so watch out!

Oxeye Daisy has a yellow center, which is the flower, while the petals are called rays.

Buttercup blooms all summer. It has long been said that when held under your chin, the flower can foretell your love of butter if it reflects yellow on your skin.

Queen Anne's Lace is also known as wild carrot. When the flower wilts, it curls up and looks like a bird's nest.

Saint-John's-Wort is seen in flower clusters and blooms all summer along the roadside.

Mountain Mint has white flowers and a wonderful mint smell (if you rub the flower head between your fingers).

This plant isn't really this big!

Trumpet Creeper is a favorite of hummingbirds. It's easy to see how it got its name.

Who's that sleepy head?

Canada Goldenrod blooms from July to September and for many people signals the beginning of allergy season.

Animals

may share your campsite, but most are very shy and hard to see. So find a quiet spot to watch and listen. An important first skill of a good naturalist is observation.

Both early morning and dusk are great times to spot moose, deer, or rabbits. Other mammals, such as bears, badgers, and raccoons, appear only after dark. You might see their eyes reflecting your campfire as they pass by in the distance. If you spot bright yellow eyes, chances are it's a raccoon. Smaller mammals, insects, and reptiles are easier to spot during the day, although they are often camouflaged for safety, so watch carefully.

Hey, I'm flying!

A White-tailed Deer is easily identified by the flash of the white underside of its tail.

Who is hiding in this picture?
The Forest Wolf Spider hides in forest litter by day and hunts at night.

A Red Squirrel is small and rusty red. It can be mistaken for a chipmunk. Living in the forest, it keeps up a noisy chatter that can be heard all year long.

TRY IT!

Carry a small magnifying insect box with you to get a closer look at small creatures around camp. Remember to always be gentle and return these little neighbors to their habitat quickly.

This wild-looking caterpillar is a common **Dagger Moth**. It feeds on poplar and willow trees. The black hair tufts are called pencils.

A **Striped Skunk** is nocturnal and eats many things, such as small mammals, fruit, and insects.

A **Raccoon** wears a black bandit face mask.

A **White-tailed Jackrabbit** is really considered a hare because it has such long ears and is larger than a rabbit.

A **Wood Frog**, with its robber's mask patch behind its eyes, lives in moist, wooded areas and makes a noise like a duck.

Animal Tracks

Animal Tracks are another great way to observe any wildlife that may be sharing your campsite. Here are their signs:

1. **Footprints** are easy to spot, especially in mud or sandy earth. If you look carefully you'll be surprised just how many creatures leave their prints behind.

2. **Gnawed Pinecones and Nuts** left by birds, squirrels, and chipmunks are often found under trees.

3. **Trimmed Trees or Bushes** usually mean that deer have been dining, especially if the trees have their lower limbs nibbled to the same height.

4. **Nuts** (not near a nut tree) can indicate that birds or squirrels have carried them a distance from their origin. Maybe there is a nest nearby.

5. **Feathers** can tell you what birds might be in the neighborhood.

Emma's Notes

I sometimes make a drawing of the footprints I see around the campsite. Then I match them up with the animal tracks in my guidebook.

Tracking

is being able to follow an animal's path. Once you have learned what a track looks like, you can begin to observe how an animal travels. The size and placement of each print will help to determine whether you are following a big or small animal. Small animals often put one foot right in front of another. Check for claw marks. You can also determine whether an animal is walking or running just by looking at the distance and depth of the prints.

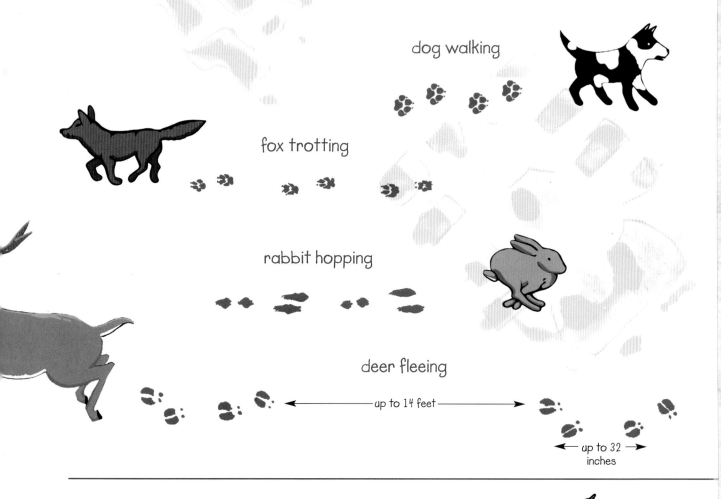

dog walking

fox trotting

rabbit hopping

deer fleeing

up to 14 feet

up to 32 inches

If your campsite is near a trail, there may be horseback riders also using that trail. Horses often change gaits, which makes their tracks interesting to follow and study.

horse walking

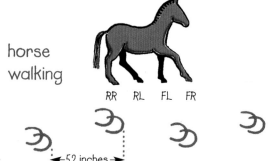

RR RL FL FR

52 inches

easure Hunt Game

Use the tracking symbols below, or make up your own, to lay a trail for your friends and family. Give everyone a list of the symbols and what each means. Then let them find their way to the treasure. Stay close to the campsite in case someone loses the trail. Always use rocks, sticks, and other natural debris to lay your trail.

this way

this way

this way

hidden note

danger

two paces this way

turn right

turn left

wait here

end of trail or go home

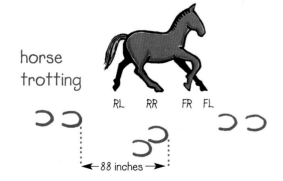

horse trotting

RL   RR   FR   FL

←— 88 inches —→

horse galloping

RL   RR   FR   FL

←— 48 to 80 —→
inches

Sounds

are all around when you are camping. If you live in the city, it's often the noise of cars that fills your ears. But when you're in the woods, you'll hear the sounds of nature and—in particular—birds. Each bird has its own distinct call, and some birdlike sounds are not birds at all. Here are some familiar sounds and their callers:

Hairy Woodpecker looks like the Downy Woodpecker, only bigger. It can be heard tapping on trees looking for insects, or making a high "peek" and a low fast rattle when it sings.

The brilliant red **Northern Cardinal** male, often seen perched atop a tree, whistles a loud "cheer, cheer" or "purty, purty, purty."

Cicadas are common insects in the heat of the summer. They make a sound easily mistaken for a bird: a high-pitched and constant rising and falling "tr-r-r-r-ill."

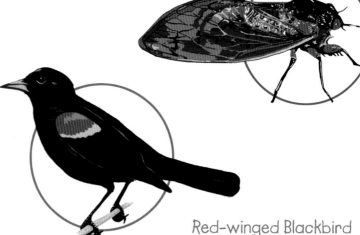

Black-capped Chickadee's "chicka-dee-dee-dee" can be heard any month of the year.

Red-winged Blackbird males have bright red markings on their wings. The sound "konk-la-ree" or "o-ka-lay" is heard often in spring.

Spring Peeper has a cross on its back and a high piping whistle, which can be heard in swampy areas after dark in the spring. Listen carefully— it's actually a frog!

Blue Jay has a black necklace and white spots on its wings and tail. "Jay, jay" is the call you hear, especially near bird feeders.

Barn Swallow has a deeply forked tail. The call is a constant twittering as the swallow flits through the sky.

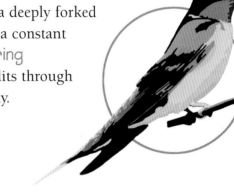

Robin, with its red breast, has a high-pitched "yeep," followed by "chuck-chuck-chuck."

And don't forget your binoculars.

You might just catch a glimpse of the creatures you hear.

American Goldfinch, visible in the summer, has a roller-coaster flight and a canarylike twittering song.

Chipmunks rustle in the trees. Their high-pitched chattering sounds like a bird, but don't be fooled.

Weather

Weather is extremely important when camping. A weather band radio can forecast what is coming, or you can look for signs in nature that predict changes in the weather. It's not always easy to read the signs, but it is fun to try.

Cumulus clouds are huge white heaps that change shape as they float by. They sometimes look like recognizable objects and are fair-weather clouds.

Thunderheads are created when cumulus clouds group together. Be careful; these massive clouds bring thunder and lightning storms, hail and flash floods.

Stratocumulus are thin layers of gray clouds that form into thicker stratus clouds.

Foul-Weather Signs:

1. Cirrus clouds develop.
2. Swelling cumulus clouds grow tall.
3. The western sky gets dark.
4. Winds come quickly from the west.
5. A ring appears around the moon.
6. Birds fly low and line up on pole wires.
7. Fishing is good.
8. Flies bite.
9. Pinecones close.
10. Dandelions close.
11. Ants march in a line.

Cirrus (feathered) clouds, often called horsetails, are high-altitude ice crystals that usually indicate a storm is coming in 24 to 48 hours.

Cirrocumulus clouds, also called mackerel scales (because they look like fish scales), don't appear for very long and usually hint at a change to rainy weather.

Rain is on the way, so get out your umbrella!

Fair-Weather Signs:

1. Morning fog burns off by noon.
2. Small cumulus clouds float by in the afternoon.
3. Geese, crows, and swallows fly high.
4. Fishing is poor.
5. Pinecones open.
6. Dandelions open.
7. Ants scurry.

TRY IT!

Cricket Chirps

Scientists know that a cricket chirps faster as the day gets hotter. You can calculate the actual temperature by counting the chirps.

1. Count the number of chirps the cricket makes in 15 seconds.

2. Add 40 to this number. The answer is the temperature in Fahrenheit.

Emma's cricket chirped 35 times in 15 seconds. What's the answer?

The answer is 75° Fahrenheit.

chirp chirp chirp

31

Rainy Days

are inevitable, so don't be gloomy. Just think of them as another adventure, and come prepared to stay dry. Have a reliable rain fly (or outer waterproof covering) for your tent, waterproof covering for your equipment, and good rain gear for yourself, including a wool or fleece sweater. A dining tarp helps to make cooking and eating easier, too.

Pack some things to help you stay busy inside the tent. Read a good book, play cards or a travel game, work on a journal, make up songs, or tell spooky stories. One of our favorite activities is practicing knot tying. You only need rope.

Knot tying is not as important to us as it was to our pioneering ancestors, but there are many reasons to know a few good knots when you are camping. See if your camping companions can name each knot you make.

Sheet Bend

The sheet bend is good for tying together ropes of different thicknesses.

1. Make a loop in the thicker rope.

2. Pass the end of the thinner rope through the loop.

3. Wrap this end behind the loop.

4. Pass the rope end under itself, back inside the loop, and tighten.

Taut-line Hitch

The taut-line hitch is a loop that can be adjusted to be larger or smaller but holds secure under tension.

1. Make a loop with the end of a rope.

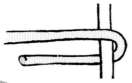

2. Loop the end twice around the other part of the rope, moving in.

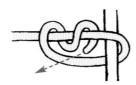

3. Make another loop away from the first two loops. Pull the end through this loop to finish the hitch.

4. Pull the hitch tight and adjust.

Bowline

The bowline makes a loop that won't close up when pulled, which is good for attaching a loop to an object. To remember this knot say: The rabbit comes out of the hole, around a tree, and ducks back into the hole. Your turn!

1. Make an overhand loop with the standing part of the rope. That is the hole.

2. Push the free end of the rope through this loop. That is the rabbit coming out of the hole.

3. Loop the rope behind the straight piece (the tree), pull it through the first overhand loop, and tighten.

Miller's Knot

The miller's knot is a good choice for tying up your bear bag.

1. Make an overhand loop 6 inches or so below the top of the bag.

2. Loop the free end around the bag a second time on top of first loop.

3. Pull it through the first overhand loop and tighten.

Campfires

can be the focal point of a campsite, though they do break the leave-no-trace rule. They are, however, sometimes necessary for cooking and keeping warm, but more often they bring the group together to relax, sing songs, tell stories, or watch the bright, dancing flames. Campfires illuminate the darkness and give your clothes that great smoky smell, which lingers long after you have gone home. If campfires are allowed, and a fire ring is available, here's how to build a campfire of your own:

This is getting heavy!

First check with the campground to see if wood is provided. If not, you'll need to find some. Be sure to use small, dry, dead wood that is already on the ground. Never take branches from standing trees (dead or alive) or remove their bark.

There are three types of wood to gather:

1. Tinder—dry leaves, twigs, pinecones, and paper that will catch on fire quickly. You can purchase firestarters to do this job, too.

2. Kindling—bigger twigs and sticks that will build the fire.

3. Fuel—small logs that will keep the fire burning.

Keep these three separate piles near your fire (but not too close). Now you are ready to build a fire. Try one of the three styles on the next page. Each is designed differently and provides the two main ingredients for a good fire: WOOD and AIR! Every fire needs to breathe, so don't smother it with too much wood.

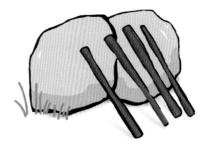

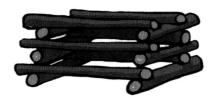

Tepee Fire. Plant a thick piece of kindling in the center of the fire ring so it can stand on its own. Place tinder around the base of the pole and stand kindling in the shape of a tepee. Light the fire and add more wood.

Log Cabin Fire. Start with a tepee fire. When the tepee has burned down, lay two large pieces of wood on opposite sides of the tepee. Lay two more pieces opposite the first two to form a square. Add two or three more layers of smaller logs. The space between layers leaves room for air circulation.

Lean-to Fire. Start with a big log or large rocks. Pile tinder and kindling against the log or rock and then lean larger sticks against the base to form a right angle. As the fire burns you can continue to lean more sticks on the base. This fire is good for windy days since the rocks act as a barrier. After it has burned down to hot coals, you can add a second rock or large log opposite the first and rest pots and pans across the top to start cooking.

Don't forget to put out the fire!

Keep a safe distance away while you dribble water from your hand on the fire. Do not pour water quickly, because sparks may flare up. Once the flame is gone, stir the coals with a stick and continue to sprinkle water until there is no more steam rising from the ring. Before you leave, carefully feel the ashes to make sure the fire is completely out.

CAMPFIRE RULES

1. Check if fires are allowed at your campsite. A forest fire can start if an area is too dry.

2. Set your fire in an established fire ring or fire pan in an area clear of plant debris and away from trees.

3. Never leave a fire unattended.

4. Have a bucket of sand or water near-by in case your fire gets too big.

5. Make sure your fire is completely out before you leave the campsite or go to bed.

6. Small fires are best for cooking and for the environment.

7. Stay upwind of your fire, so smoke and sparks don't hit you, and wear long pants to prevent getting burned.

Time to Eat.

Food always tastes better when you're camping. Remember to take time to plan your meals before you go. Pack lightly. For example, take a bag of cereal instead of a box and avoid canned goods. You can also buy freeze-dried meals that are lightweight. There are many great camping recipes to try, but here are a few of Emma and Lydia's favorites.

Food Starters.

Keep ingredients nutritional and simple, at least for your first trip, and take along a lot of energy staples such as:

- peanut butter
- jelly
- crackers
- fruit leathers
- apples
- pasta
- rice
- nuts
- dried fruit
- carrots
- celery
- pancake mix
- raisin bread
- energy bars
- cereal
- dry soup
- hot and cold powdered drink mixes

Gorp.

The name stands for Good Ole Raisins and Peanuts, but everyone knows it as trail mix. Below is a list of possibilities. Experiment with your own ingredients.

Ingredients:

Peanuts

Nuts of any kind

Raisins (plain, chocolate, or yogurt-covered)

M&M's or chocolate chips

Dried fruit, such as dates, apricots, bananas, apples, and pineapples

Sunflower seeds

Granola or other cereal

Shredded coconut

Twist Biscuit.

You can make a variety of biscuits and breads either with a prepared mix or by mixing the ingredients from scratch.

Well, I like mine a little burned!

I like mine lightly toasted.

Ingredients:

4 cups all-purpose flour	1 tsp. salt
1/4 cup dry skim milk	3/4 stick margarine
8 tsp. baking powder	1 cup water

1. Combine all dry ingredients. Then mix in the margarine, and finally the water. (You can premix the dry ingredients before the trip.)
2. Use a stick about two feet long and two inches wide. Peel off the bark.
3. Warm the stick by the fire and then wet it with water.
4. Roll the dough into a snake and twist it around the stick.
5. Push the end of the stick into the ground, so that the dough can bake on its own, or hold the stick over the fire and turn it occasionally to brown all sides.

Campfire Stew.

If you make this stew with meat, plan to have it the first night while the meat is still fresh.

Ingredients:

2 lbs. ground beef	1 onion, diced
salt and pepper	2 cans condensed vegetable soup

Options: Rice and/or canned pinto beans

1. Season ground beef with salt and pepper, and mix thoroughly.
2. Roll meat into small balls.
3. Cook the meat and onion in a large pot over the fire or a camp stove until the meat is well browned and the onions are translucent.
4. Add vegetable soup and enough water to keep it from sticking.
5. Cover and cook slowly for 20 to 25 minutes.

Options:

1. Cook whole-grain rice separately and pour stew over the rice for an extra-hearty meal.
2. For a meatless solution try the same meal, substituting pinto beans for the ground beef.

S'mores

S'mores are really sweet and gooey. Lydia eats two, but I can only eat one. How many can you eat?

Ingredients:
1 graham cracker
1/2 chocolate bar
1 marshmallow

1. Break the cracker in half.
2. Place chocolate on one half of the graham cracker.
3. Cook your marshmallow on a stick over the campfire until it's golden brown.
4. Put marshmallow on top of chocolate and cover with the other graham cracker half.
5. Eat and enjoy.

Games

that don't require any special equipment are great for a camping trip. Here are some that Emma, Lydia, and their friends like to play while out in the woods.

Go in, go in!

1. Cup Toss

Collect two or three cups and three small stones or pinecones. Place the cups in a line on level ground. Everyone take three steps back from the cups and one at a time toss an item into a cup. Take another step back and toss again. Continue to step away with each toss. Count the number of times you get your item into a cup.

I can do it!

2. Blindfold Touch

One person is blindfolded with a bandanna. A second person hands the blindfolded person objects to touch from around the camp. After touching each object, the person tries to guess what the object is. When the guesser misses, a new person is blindfolded.

3. Treasure Hunt

You can use a combination of camp equipment and natural objects to create a list of ten items. Divide the group into two or more teams. Each team gets a list of items and has 20 minutes to bring those items back to a designated spot. The team with the most items after 20 minutes wins. When choosing nature items, only pick up ground litter such as pinecones, fallen leaves, and sticks that you can put back. Don't disturb living things.

You got me!

4. Flashlight Tag

This is a game for **AFTER DARK.**

The person who is "it" stands in one place and tries to tag the other players with the light of a flashlight. If you are tagged, then you become the flashlight holder. The players must stay within sight of the campsite. Running is discouraged for safety.

5. Jump the Creek

Place two sticks about 2 feet apart. Stand in front of one stick and jump over both sticks. When everyone has jumped, move the sticks a little farther apart. The sticks cannot be moved until everyone has made it across. If one player has trouble, then the others must help that player get across.

6. Story Round

This is a great game to play around a campfire. The first person begins a story and may at any moment stop. The next person continues the story in any way he or she chooses. The story continues around the whole group until someone decides to bring it to an end.

Peep Peep
Peep Peep
says the Peeper Frog sitting in the
wetland bog.

Night is a time for us to rest. But for other
creatures, it is time to hunt for food. Snuggle into
your warm sleeping bag and listen carefully to the
different sounds you hear before falling asleep.

Chica - Chica -
Chic - Chic
says the Horny Toad from the reeds
of the shimmering stream bank.

Chirp -
Chirp -
Chirp
says the Cricket from
a mossy patch under the
oak tree.

Eee - Eee - Eee - Eee

says the Brown Bat darting through
the air searching for mosquitoes.

Wha Wha Wha - Whoo - Whoo

says the Great Horned Owl
from the old dark oak tree looming
above our tent.

Burr Burr
    Burr Burr

says the Buck Deer
standing in the clearing
behind our campsite.

Did
you hear
something?

Arcturus

To the west is the bright orange star
Arcturus, which forms the bottom
point of a kite-shaped constellation.
This kite is known as The Herdsman,
or Bootes.

The Herdsman
(Bootes)

Stars begin to appear as soon
as the sun goes down. When the sky
grows darker the little points of light
become more numerous. In the
wilderness, away from city lights, you
can see millions of stars on a clear
night. You may also see planets.
Venus is the first visible light in the
evening on the western horizon, and
Mars is usually a small red dot low
in the sky. Falling meteors, known
as shooting stars, streak across with
a tail of light, and satellites appear as
small specks moving steadily in a
straight line overhead. Don't forget to
look for constellations. Here are a
few of the easiest to see in the summer sky. Find an open area near
your campsite and spend some time
looking up.

Big Dipper
(in Ursa Major)

The Big Dipper got
its name from a long-
handled ladle used
to scoop water in
pioneer times.

You can follow the two ladle end
points of the Big Dipper to find the
North Star and the ladle end of the
Little Dipper.

◄ The small crown shape
is Northern Crown
(Corona Borealis).

The Summer Triangle is easy to
see because it's made up of
three bright stars: Vega, Altair,
and Deneb.

Altair

Vega

Deneb

Shooting Star
(Meteorite)

Little Dipper
(in Ursa Minor)

Cassiopeia looks
like a wiggly W.

North Star

I see a
shooting
star!

Time to Go.

Sooner or later it's time to clean up the campsite and think about heading home. Everyone works to roll up the tent. Europa packs her belongings into a backpack and helps Zachary gather the garbage into bags. The latrine is filled in, Emma checks that the fire ring is cold, Lydia shakes out her sleeping bag, and Bobby takes down the bear bag. Everyone double-checks that nothing is left behind, because they remember the most important rule of camping:

A good camper always leaves a campsite looking like no one was there. Leave no trace!

After we hike back to our car, a stop at an ice-cream stand on our way home makes the perfect ending to a great camping trip!

Don't go yet, because it's time to take . . .

The Master Camper Certification Quiz

☑ Answer the following questions correctly, and you can sign your name to the **Master Camper Certificate** on the next page and officially call yourself a master camper. If you miss a few, read the book again and have another try.

1. What is the most important rule of camping?

- ○ a. Don't walk on the grass
- ○ b. Always wear a scarf
- ○ c. Leave no trace
- ○ d. Eat lots of marshmallows

2. What two items are used to navigate on a trail?

- ○ a. Flashlight
- ○ b. Compass
- ○ c. Map
- ○ d. Rope

3. Where should the latrine be located at a campsite?

- ○ a. Four inches from your tent
- ○ b. Under a rock
- ○ c. Next to a river or lake
- ○ d. 200 feet from a river or lake

4. What item should you have with you in case you get lost?

- ○ a. Whistle
- ○ b. Set of keys
- ○ c. Toothbrush
- ○ d. Pair of clean socks

5. What is a bear bag?

- ○ a. A place to store a bear
- ○ b. A place to store food to feed a bear
- ○ c. A place to store food so that a bear can't reach it
- ○ d. A fancy sleeping bag

6. What is the Big Dipper?

- ○ a. The name of your favorite ice cream
- ○ b. A cooking spoon
- ○ c. A bird
- ○ d. A constellation

7. Why does a woodpecker make a tap-tap-tapping noise in the trees?

- ○ **a.** To call home
- ○ **b.** To find insects in the tree
- ○ **c.** To sharpen its beak
- ○ **d.** To make music

8. Which is usually a night sound?

- ○ **a.** Chicka-dee-dee
- ○ **b.** Jay, jay
- ○ **c.** Cheer, cheer
- ○ **d.** Wha-whoo-whoo

9. What kind of creature can often forecast the weather?

- ○ **a.** Cricket
- ○ **b.** Squirrel
- ○ **c.** Parrot
- ○ **d.** Snake

10. How many s'mores can Emma eat?

- ○ **a.** Seven
- ○ **b.** Three
- ○ **c.** One
- ○ **d.** One hundred!

MASTER CAMPER CERTIFICATE

This document certifies that _____
(Your name here)

has earned the title of Master Camper. The above-named

individual is hereby recognized as an official outdoor

explorer and camper. This certificate entitles you to one

fun hike with the friend (or parent) of your choice.

Emma and Lydia's Final Word

Congratulations! You are a true master camper. We sure hope you've enjoyed our camping trip; now you are ready to set out on your own. Good luck, and maybe we'll see you in the woods!

So long!

THE EMMA AND LYDIA SEAL OF APPROVAL

Sources and Resources

Organizations

American Canoe Association (ACA)
7432 Alban Station Boulevard
Suite B-232
Springfield, VA 22150
703-451-0141
www.aca-paddler.org

American Hiking Society (AHS)
1422 Fenwick Lane
Silver Spring, MD 20910
301-565-6704
www.americanhiking.org

Appalachian Mountain Club (AMC)
5 Joy Street
Boston, MA 02108
617-523-0636
www.outdoors.org
Offers many family-oriented programs. AMC huts are a great way to start children backpacking.

The Nature Conservancy
4245 North Fairfax Drive, Suite 100
Arlington, VA 22203
800-628-6860
www.tnc.org
Responsible for the preservation of millions of acres of land full of trails ideal for family hikes.

Sierra Club
85 Second Street, Second Floor
San Francisco, CA 94105
415-977-5500
www.sierraclub.org
A long-standing national organization that offers trips, programs, and publications for families.

Tour Organizers

Backroads
801 Cedar Street
Berkeley, CA 94710
800-462-2848
www.backroads.com

American Youth Hostels
733 15th Street N.W., Suite 840
Washington, DC 20005
202-783-6161
www.hiayh.org

Magazines

Backpacker
Rodale Press
33 East Minor Street
Emmaus, PA 18098
610-967-8296
www.bpbasecamp.com

Canoe & Kayak
10526 N.E. 68th Street, Suite 3
Kirkland, WA 98033
425-827-6363
canoekayak.about.com

Outside
400 Market Street
Santa Fe, NM 87501
505-989-7100
outsidemag.com